MILITARY VEHICLES

U.S.
NAVY
AIRCRAFT CARRIERS

by Carrie A. Braulick

Reading Consultant
Barbara J. Fox
Reading Specialist
North Carolina State University

Capstone
press

Mankato, Minnesota

Blazers is published by Capstone Press,
151 Good Counsel Drive, P.O. Box 669, Mankato, Minnesota 56002.
www.capstonepress.com

Library of Congress Cataloging-in-Publication Data
Braulick, Carrie A., 1975–
    U.S. Navy aircraft carriers / by Carrie A. Braulick.
    p. cm.—(Blazers—military vehicles)
    Summary: "Provides an overview of the design, use, weapons,
and equipment of U.S. Navy aircraft carriers"—Provided by publisher.
    Includes bibliographical references and index.
    ISBN-13: 978-0-7368-5470-2 (hardcover)
    ISBN-10: 0-7368-5470-3 (hardcover)
    1. Aircraft carriers—United States—Juvenile literature. 2. United
States. Navy—Equipment and supplies—Juvenile literature. I. Title. II.
Series.
V874.3.B73 2006
623.825'5'0973—dc22   2005016448

Editorial Credits
Tom Adamson, editor; Thomas Emery, designer; Jo Miller,
    photo researcher/photo editor

Photo Credits
Corbis/Reuters/US Navy/Corey Lewis, 13 (bottom); US Navy/PH2
    Tracy Lee Didas, 19; Jason P. Taylor, 18
DVIC/PH1 Jim Hampshire, 28–29
Getty Images Inc./Koichi Kamoshida, 14; Sandy Huffaker, 26 (top)
Photo by Ted Carlson/Fotodynamics, cover; 10, 22–23
U.S. Navy Photo by PHAN Chris M. Valdez, 5; PH2 Matthew J. MaGee,
    6; PH3 Joshua Word, 9; PHAN Ryan O'Connor, 11; PH2 Jomo K.
    Coffea, 12; PHAN Brad Garner, 13 (top); Paul Farley, 15; PHAN
    Philip A. McDaniel, 17; PH3 Matthew Bash, 20; PHAN Christopher
    Molinari, 21; PHAN Jordon R. Beesley, 25; PHAN Grantez
    Stephens, 26 (bottom)

**Capstone Press thanks the U.S. Navy Office of Information East for
    their help in preparing this book.**

1 2 3 4 5 6 11 10 09 08 07 06

TABLE OF CONTENTS

NAVY AIRCRAFT CARRIERS

A U.S. Navy aircraft carrier is a powerful force at sea. Fighter planes patrol the sky above each carrier.

Aircraft carriers are huge. They are the largest warships ever built. They carry up to 85 airplanes. The crew lives on the ship for months at a time.

BLAZER FACT

An aircraft carrier is as long as three football fields.

DESIGN

Many levels, or decks, make up each aircraft carrier. The top deck is the flight deck. Fighter planes soar off the end of the flight deck.

ISLAND

An island sticks up from the flight
deck. Crew members in the island steer
the carrier. They keep track of airplanes
on the flight deck.

HANGAR DECK

Planes are stored and fixed on the large hangar deck. In the Combat Direction Center, crew members send planes out to defend the ship.

COMBAT DIRECTION CENTER

PROPELLER

14

Most carriers have nuclear reactors. These devices power the engines. Four large propellers push a carrier through the water.

WEAPONS AND EQUIPMENT

Fighter planes are a carrier's best weapons. These fast planes are loaded with guns, bombs, and missiles.

Other ships sail with each carrier. They provide extra protection against enemy attacks. Carriers also have their own guns and missiles.

SEA SPARROW MISSILE SYSTEM

CARRIER STRIKE GROUP

BLAZER FACT

An aircraft carrier and the ships around it is called a carrier strike group.

LCDR NICK ANDERSON
"NIPS"

20

AT3 RYAN DANOSKI
"DANO"
KENOSHA, WI

CATAPULT

A catapult shoots the plane off the
flight deck. An arresting wire stops the
plane when it lands. A hook on the plane
catches the wire.

BLAZER FACT

A catapult pushes an airplane to 100 miles (161 kilometers) per hour in less than 3 seconds.

★ ★ ★ ★ ★ ★

ARRESTING WIRE

HULL

ISLAND

FLIGHT DECK

CLOSE-IN WEAPONS SYSTEM

ABOARD AIRCRAFT CARRIERS

A carrier has about 5,500 crew members. About 3,000 sailors run the carrier. Another 2,500 members make up the air wing. They fly and fix the planes.

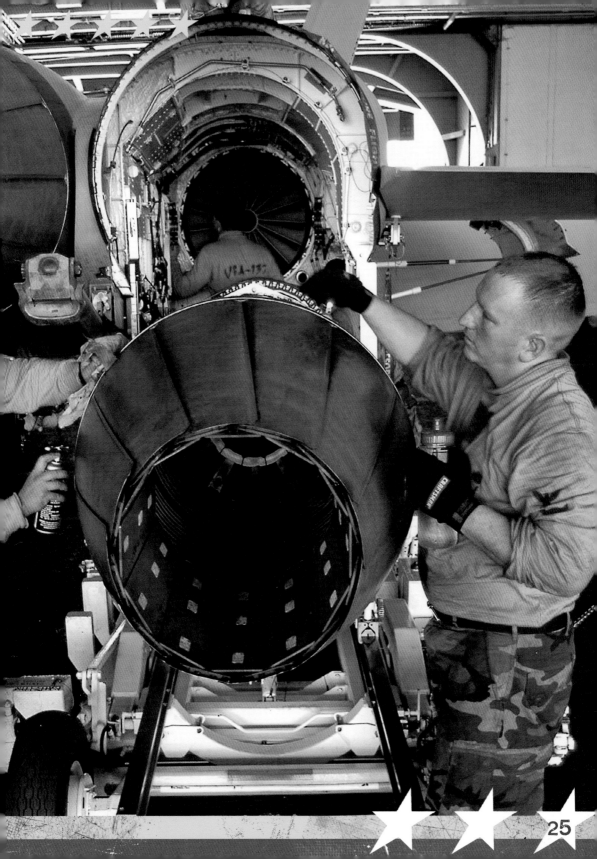

MESS DECK

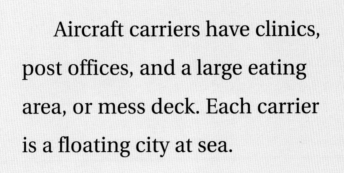

Aircraft carriers have clinics, post offices, and a large eating area, or mess deck. Each carrier is a floating city at sea.

BLAZER FACT

Cooks on a carrier serve 18,000 meals a day.

HOMEWARD BOUND!

GLOSSARY

arresting wire (uh-REST-ing WIRE)—a long, thin, flexible piece of metal used to stop planes that are landing on an aircraft carrier

catapult (KAT-uh-pult)—a device that launches planes off a carrier's flight deck

deck (DEK)—a level on an aircraft carrier; aircraft carriers have several decks, including the flight deck and hangar deck.

hull (HUHL)—the main body of a ship

island (EYE-luhnd)—the area on a carrier's flight deck where the captain and crew operate the ship

mess deck (MESS DEK)—the eating area on an aircraft carrier

nuclear reactor (NOO-klee-ur ree-AK-tur)— a device that makes nuclear power; aircraft carriers run on nuclear power.

propeller (pruh-PEL-ur)—a set of rotating blades that pushes a ship through the water

READ MORE

Doeden, Matt. *The U.S. Navy.* The U.S. Armed Forces. Mankato, Minn.: Capstone Press, 2005.

Doyle, Kevin. *Aircraft Carriers.* Military Hardware in Action. Minneapolis: Lerner, 2003.

Stone, Lynn M. *Aircraft Carriers.* Fighting Forces on the Sea. Vero Beach, Fla.: Rourke, 2006.

INTERNET SITES

FactHound offers a safe, fun way to find Internet sites related to this book. All of the sites on FactHound have been researched by our staff.

Here's how:

1. Visit *www.facthound.com*
2. Type in this special code **0736854703** for age-appropriate sites. Or enter a search word related to this book for a more general search.
3. Click on the **Fetch It** button.

FactHound will fetch the best sites for you!

INDEX

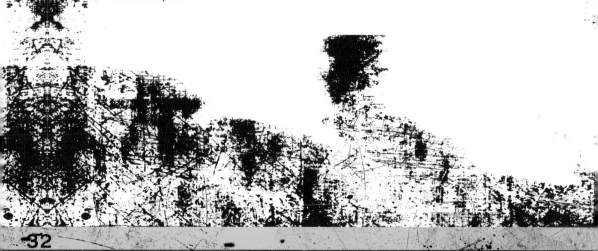